WARNING

THE AUTHOR OF THIS BOOK PREFERS TO REMAIN HIDDEN BECAUSE SHE KNOWS ALL THE SECRETS ABOUT THE ENCHANTING POWERS OF BOOKS...BUT ALSO BECAUSE SHE SOMETIMES WRITES COMPLETE NONSENSE

SUPER SHADES

AWESOME WIG

OUTFIT BY RENTABODY

WORDS AND DRAWINGS BY
FRANÇOIZE BOUCHER

WALKER BOOKS FOR YOUNG READERS
AN IMPRINT OF BLOOMSBURY
NEW YORK LONDON NEW DELHI SYDNEY

READING MAKES YOU **GROW** (MUCH FASTER THAN EATING VEGETABLES). IT'S A WELL-KNOWN FACT THAT IF YOU GET TO BE **100** AND YOU'RE STILL READING, YOU'LL JUST KEEP ON GROWING!

READING

INCREASES YOUR
VOCABULARY,
IMPROVES THE WAY
YOU **SPEAK,**
AND MAKES YOUR
CONVERSATION
ABSOLUTELY
IRRESISTIBLE

→

PROOF

GIMME THE SALT!

BEFORE READING BOOKS

DAAAAHLING, IF IT'S NOT TOO MUCH TROUBLE WOULD YOU BE SO KIND AS TO PASS ME THE SODIUM CHLORIDE, SO THAT I CAN SPRINKLE SOME ON MY FRENCH FRIES? THANK YOU SO MUCH.

AFTER READING BOOKS

READING WON'T MAKE YOU FAT

3 LAYERS OF SHEET CAKE

1000 CALORIES

So make sure you polish off books rather than cakes and junk food!

CAN YOU GET SICK IF YOU READ TOO MUCH?

HOSPITAL PATIENT SUFFERING FROM ACUTE READINGITIS (AFTER READING **20** NOVELS AND **12** COMIC BOOKS)

ANSWER

NOT NORMALLY, BUT
WATCH OUT!

BECAUSE IN EXTREME CASES YOU COULD ACTUALLY DIE FROM IT!

TURN OVER QUICKLY
TO FIND OUT HOW

PROOF: THIS PERSON DIED
LAUGHING LAST NIGHT WHILE
READING A **FUNNY** BOOK

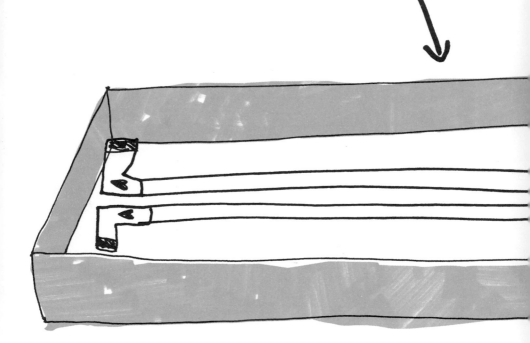

HAHAHA !!!

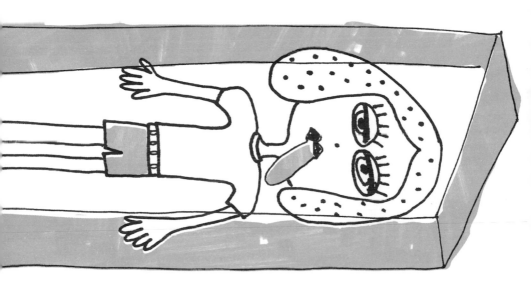

IT'S TOO LATE FOR HER,
BUT NOT FOR YOU,
SO WATCH OUT!

IF YOU LOVE A BOOK YOU CAN
READ IT OVER AND OVER
**THOUSANDS
OF TIMES**

BUT,
IF YOU LOVE CHOCOLATE,
YOU CAN ONLY EAT
THE SAME BAR ONCE

PROOF

BEFORE

AFTER

WHEN YOU'VE
EATEN IT ALL

↓

THERE'S NOTHING LEFT

WHEN YOU'VE
READ IT ALL

↓

IT'S STILL
THERE!

You can PRETEND YOU'RE SOMEBODY ELSE, ESCAPE FROM REALITY, AND HAVE AWESOME ADVENTURES

READING DEVELOPS YOUR IMAGINATION

YOU, AFTER YOU'VE READ
BOOKS ABOUT SUPERHEROES

YOUR HOUSE

VERY SMALL ADVERTISEMENT

IN VIEW OF THE **CRAZY NUMBER** OF PEOPLE WHO WILL SEE THIS BOOK, THE AUTHOR TAKES THE OPPORTUNITY TO POST A SMALL ADVERTISEMENT THAT HAS NOTHING WHATSOEVER TO DO WITH THE BOOK!

LOST
3 MONTHS AGO

HANDBAG CONTAINING
A MILLION DOLLARS AND A
GRILLED-CHEESE SANDWICH

IF FOUND, PLEASE RING
555-1212

BOOKS CAN MAKE YOU FEEL SO MANY **DIFFERENT EMOTIONS** LIKE:

HAPPINESS

DISAPPOINTMENT

EQUIPMENT FOR READING A SAD BOOK TO KEEP FROM DROWNING IN YOUR OWN TEARS

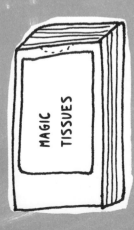

MAGIC TISSUES

ANGER

FEAR

LOVE

WONDER

SADNESS

...AND LOTS MORE!

IT'S TRULY **AMAZING!!!**

YOU CAN READ
IN ANY WEATHER

WHEN IT'S **RAINING**

WHEN IT'S **SNOWING**

WHEN IT'S **TOO HOT**

THIS IS
A MIRAGE

WHEN IT'S -13 DEGREES

AND THIS IS
A HALLUCINATION

DURING A **HURRICANE**

OR A **TORNADO**

NEEDS CHECKING

NO NEED TO LOOK
AT THE FORECAST

WHEN YOU'RE FEELING COLD (OR SAD), SOME BOOKS CAN **CHEER YOU UP**

WARM, COZY INTERIOR

STORY STUFFED FULL OF LOVE AND WARMTH

HAPPY ← ENDING!

↑ 100% CASHMERE COVER

EVEN THE ABOMINABLE SNOWMAN WANTS ONE!

BRRRRR!

A BOOK CAN SAVE YOUR DIGNITY IF SOMEBODY BARGES INTO YOUR ROOM WHEN YOU'RE STARK NAKED

⟹

SOME BOOKS
CAN MAKE YOU
SUPER
INTERESTING
AND **FASCINATING**
AND MAKE YOU
SHINE AMONG
YOUR FRIENDS

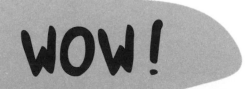

WOW!

YOU, BEFORE
READING A BOOK

YOU, AFTER READING A
GOOD BOOK!

BLAH, BLAH...
ABOUT AS
FASCINATING
AS A MUSSEL

THE PICTURE
SAYS IT ALL!

YOU SEE THE DIFFERENCE?

YOU CAN READ
**ABSOLUTELY
ANYWHERE**

EVEN ON YOUR BIKE
USING A PERISCOPE

HARRY
POTTER

HOT
STUFF!!

GOOD NEWS: A BOOK NEVER BREAKS DOWN

SOME BOOKS ARE MAGICAL!

← THE BOOK THAT TAKES ITSELF
BACK TO THE LIBRARY BEFORE THE
DUE DATE SO YOU DON'T GET A FINE

THE BOOK WITH
SELF-TURNING PAGES →

THE GLOWING BOOK YOU
CAN READ IN THE DARK

BIG SHOW-OFF!

NIGHTTIME
ADVENTURES

JEALOUS GLOWWORM

THE ELECTRIC BOOK
THAT READS TO YOU
WHEN YOU PLUG IT IN

And what's more, <u>IF YOU DON'T LIKE THIS BOOK,</u> SAY THE MAGIC WORDS TO OPEN THE SECRET PASSAGE SO YOU CAN ESCAPE NOW WITHOUT HAVING TO FINISH IT

→

MAGIC WORDS: REPEAT 3 TIMES

WHAT A STUPID BOOK!
WHAT A USELESS BOOK!
OH, I HATE THIS BOOK!

BUT THINK CAREFULLY! YOU DON'T KNOW WHERE THE SECRET PASSAGE ENDS UP! YOU MAY FIND YOURSELF **SOMEWHERE EVEN WORSE THAN THIS BOOK**, LIKE IN A SWAMP FULL OF STARVING GIANT ALLIGATORS

OR AT THE BOTTOM OF A JAR OF PICKLES

OR QUITE SIMPLY ON AN UNKNOWN PLANET

EMERGENCY EXIT

GOOD RIDDANCE

TOO LATE! YOU WERE WARNED! LOOK WHAT HAPPENED TO READERS WHO ESCAPED THROUGH THE SECRET PASSAGE

PARTIAL REMAINS OF AN UNLUCKY READER

PLANET OF STARVING MONSTERS

YOU DON'T **HAVE TO** READ THE BOOKS THAT **EVERYBODY** READS. YOU CAN READ WHAT **YOU WANT** BECAUSE YOU ARE **UNIQUE**...

BESIDES, THERE ARE BOOKS ABOUT ALL THE THINGS YOU'RE INTERESTED IN

FOR EXAMPLE,

IF YOU WANT TO KNOW WHY YOUR CAT'S IN A BAD MOOD

UNDERSTANDING MEOWS IN 10 EASY LESSONS

* TRANSLATION: THANKS...YOU FORGOT MY CAVIAR-FLAVOR DINNER AGAIN

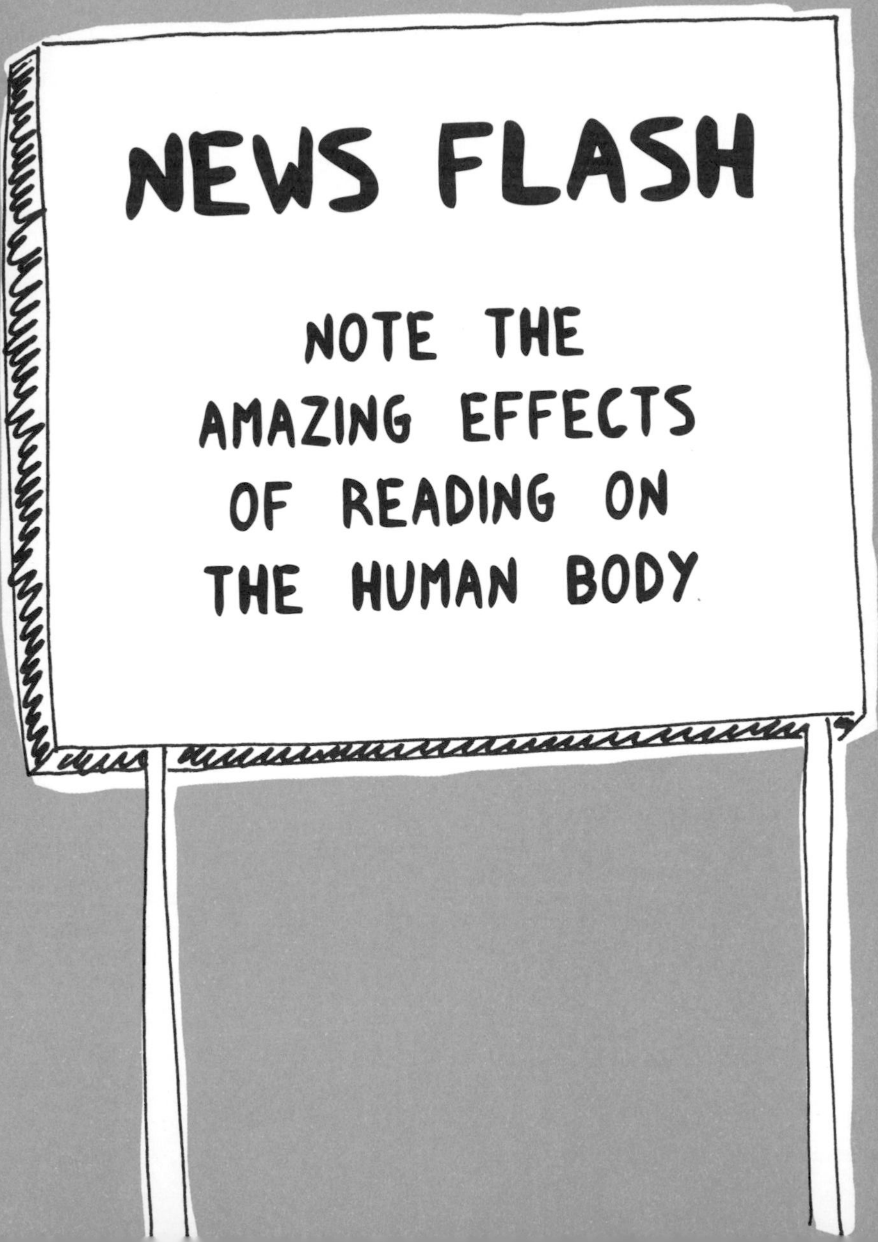

NEWS FLASH

NOTE THE
AMAZING EFFECTS
OF READING ON
THE HUMAN BODY

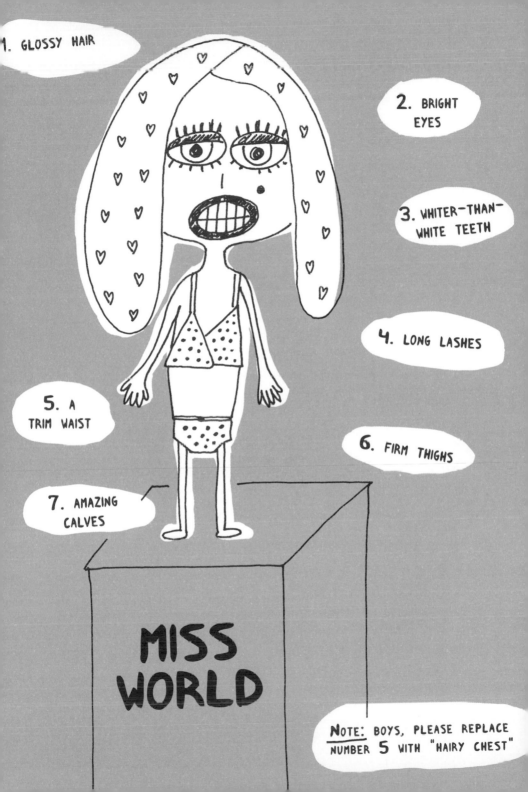

AT LEAST WITH A BOOK,

YOU NEVER LOSE

THE REMOTE CONTROL

ZAP !

ZAP!

A BOOK **NEVER** GETS AN AWFUL **VIRUS** LIKE **YOUR** **COMPUTER** DOES

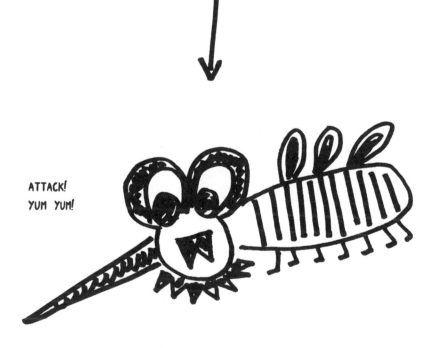

ATTACK!
YUM YUM!

SO YOU <u>NEVER NEED</u> TO CALL THE COMPUTER HELP LINE AND LOSE YOUR COOL

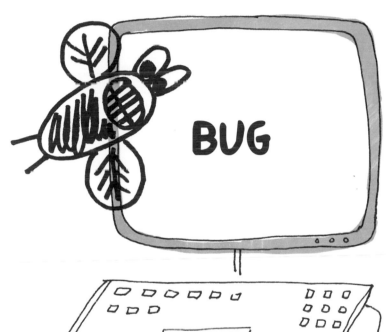

BUG

5 GOOD REASONS (WELL, 2 ARE BAD...) FOR GIVING A BOOK AS A PRESENT INSTEAD OF GIVING FLOWERS

1. NO NEED TO LOOK FOR A VASE

2. NO NEED TO CHANGE THE WATER

3. NO THORNS

4. YOU CAN READ IT FIRST (NOT VERY POLITE)

5. YOU CAN GIVE AWAY A BOOK YOU GOT AS A PRESENT BUT DON'T LIKE

ACTUALLY: FORGET THIS IDEA IF YOU DON'T WANT TO LOSE YOUR FRIENDS

WHAT'S MORE, IT WON'T WILT
LIKE THIS DAISY!

YOU CAN
SKIP PAGES

WHEN WATCHING TV,
EVERYONE HAS TO AGREE BEFORE
YOU CHANGE THE CHANNEL.
**AT LEAST WITH
A BOOK** YOU CAN TURN THE
PAGE WHENEVER YOU LIKE

YOU CAN
READ
THE END
RIGHT AWAY

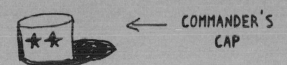

COMMANDER'S CAP ←

YOU ARE THE BOSS!

CHIEF'S HEADDRESS ↓

THE BEST PART!
YOU DON'T HAVE TO WAIT
FOR THE COMMERCIAL BREAK
TO GET AN ICE CREAM
FROM THE FREEZER!

SOMETIMES A BOOK CAN BECOME
YOUR **BEST FRIEND**

WILL NEVER LEAVE YOU

NEVER JEALOUS

TELLS YOU REALLY
INTERESTING THINGS

FUN TO BE WITH

NEVER REPEATS ITSELF

ALWAYS STRAIGHTFORWARD

100% RELIABLE
(EVEN WHEN THERE'S
A POWER OUTAGE)

WILL NEVER LET YOU DOWN

ALWAYS IN A GOOD MOOD

NEVER SULKS

UNLESS, THAT IS, YOU GO TOO FAR!

→ IT'S TRUE,
IF YOU DON'T
RESPECT A BOOK,
IT CAN
GET ANGRY!

JELLY

TOMATO
SAUCE

PEANUT
BUTTER

SOMETHING →
UNMENTIONABLE

MELTED
CHOCOLATE

**STICKY HANDS
TURNING
THE PAGES!**

GO AWAY!

WASH YOUR

GRUBBY HANDS

BEFORE YOU

TOUCH ME!

FURIOUS
BOOK

YOU'LL NEVER GET BORED IF YOU'VE GOT A GOOD BOOK

NOT LIKE THEM

IT'S SOOO
BORING IN HERE,
GET ME A BOOK!

2,000 TURNS PER MINUTE

THE SUPER INVISIBLE BOOK
(LETS YOU INVENT
THE BEST STORIES
IMAGINABLE)

1. STRETCH YOUR HANDS OUT IN FRONT OF YOU
2. CONCENTRATE REALLY HARD
3. PRETEND TO BE TURNING PAGES
4. SAY ANYTHING THAT COMES INTO YOUR HEAD (TO YOURSELF!)

EVEN BETTER THAN AN iPAD

ADVANTAGES:

1. AS LIGHT AS AIR
2. **UNLIMITED** ACCESS AND **FREE** TO DOWNLOAD

GREAT NEWS:
Books don't have an expiration date (you won't be poisoned if you read a book ages after you bought it)

$\longrightarrow$

PROOF

TODAY	IN **3** YEARS' TIME

A BRAND-NEW BOOK

STILL AS GOOD AS NEW!

A FRESHLY-LAID EGG

YUCKKK!

STINKY AND ROTTEN

A **NEW** POTATO

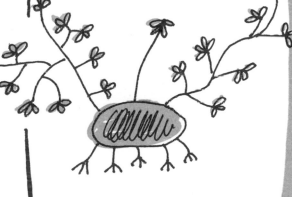

ZILLIONS OF GREEN SPROUTS

SOMETIMES, A BOOK
IS LIKE A LAMP:
IT SHEDS LIGHT ON
**LIFE'S GREAT
QUESTIONS.**

BOOKS
NEVER
MAKE
A NOISE.
THEY
LET YOU
RELAX IN
MAGNIFICENT
SILENCE

→

IRRITATING FLY WHO
DOESN'T STOP TALKING

BOOKS ARE LIKE RABBITS:
NEW ONES APPEAR EVERY DAY!

HOWEVER, BOOKS ARE BETTER THAN RABBITS BECAUSE

YOU DON'T HAVE TO CLEAN OUT THEIR CAGE EVERY MORNING

YOU DON'T HAVE TO FEED THEM EVERY 5 MINUTES

YOU DON'T HAVE TO GET SOMEONE TO TAKE CARE OF THEM WHEN YOU GO AWAY

THEY LIVE FOREVER

THEY DON'T SMELL

A BOOK CAN'T HAVE 25 BABIES IN A SINGLE NIGHT

SO ASK FOR A BOOK INSTEAD OF A RABBIT FOR YOUR BIRTHDAY!

PERSONAL MESSAGE

WOULD THE PERSON WHO LEFT
AN **OLD SOCK** IN THIS BOOK
PLEASE COME AND GET IT
IMMEDIATELY. THIS IS A
BOOK ABOUT BOOKS, NOT SOCKS!

AND WHAT'S MORE,
IT'S RUINING THE PAGE!

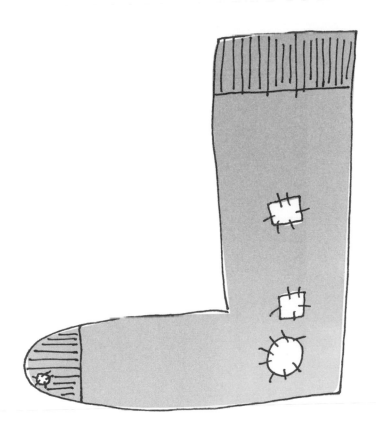

THANK YOU
XXX

ONE DAY MY PRINCE
WILL COME ON HIS
WHITE HORSE AND
HE'LL PUT HIS DIRTY
SOCKS AND UNDERWEAR
IN THE LAUNDRY
BASKET WITHOUT
BEING ASKED

100% GOLD

YOU CAN ALWAYS DREAM, THANKS TO BOOKS!

KNOWING HOW TO READ IS **FANTASTIC.** IT FEEDS YOUR BRAIN, IMPROVES THE WAY YOU THINK, AND HELPS YOU FULFILL YOUR WILDEST DREAMS

SO EVERY BOOK IS A **TREASURE CHEST** OF LEARNING

BOOK

BOOKS CAN
HELP YOUR
MIND GROW

EVERYTHING
THERE IS
TO KNOW
ABOUT
EVERYTHING

WHAT'S REALLY **GREAT** IS THAT YOU CAN EVEN READ **REALLY WEIRD** BOOKS WITHOUT ANYBODY KNOWING!

EXAMPLE :

101 USES FOR OWL POOP AND PELLETS

YOU JUST NEED TO MAKE A NEW COVER

1000 DELICIOUS COOKIE RECIPES FOR THE WHOLE FAMILY

How to do it:

1. COVER YOUR BOOK WITH
    PLAIN WHITE PAPER

2. INVENT A NEW TITLE AND
    DRAW SOMETHING RELEVANT

...AND **TA-DA!** NOBODY
IS ANY THE WISER!

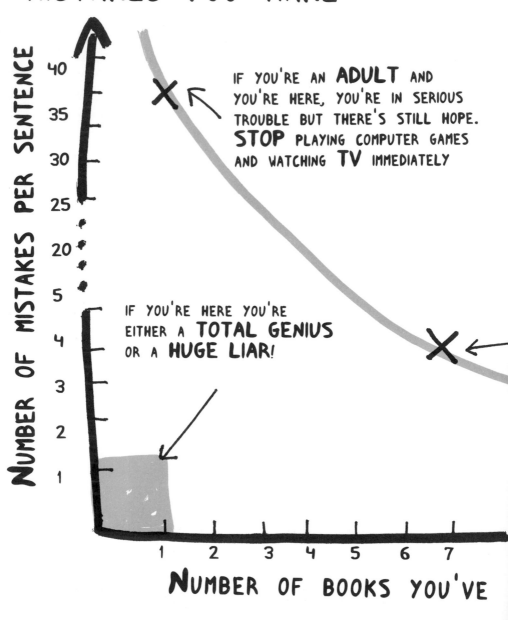

Your
IDEAL
TARGET
(YES, YOU CAN!)

IF YOU'RE **HERE**
(CHILDREN AND GROWN-UPS)
YOU CAN DO MUCH BETTER.
IT'S UP TO YOU...

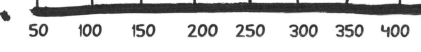

50   100   150   200   250   300   350   400

READ DURING YOUR LIFETIME

IF BIG BOOKS WITH MORE
THAN 500 PAGES
SCARE YOU,
START BY READING
TINY EASY ONES
WITH 4 PAGES

LOOK

TABLE OF COMPARISONS

CASE NUMBER 1

A BIG BOOK NEXT TO A CHERRY TOMATO
AND DOG POOP FROM A MINIATURE POODLE

CASE NUMBER 2

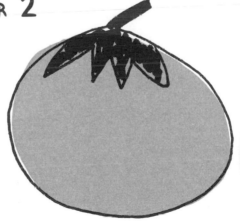

A TINY BOOK NEXT TO THE SAME TOMATO
AND THE SAME PIECE OF DOG POOP

WITH A BOOK, YOU CAN EXPLORE ALL THE COUNTRIES OF THE WORLD WITHOUT POLLUTING THE PLANET

YOU CAN EVEN BE A <u>TIME TRAVELER!</u>
HOW AWESOME IS THAT?

SO PICK UP A BOOK,

PARK YOURSELF IN THIS
ARMCHAIR AND TAKE OFF
ON AN ADVENTURE!

IT'S CHEAPER
THAN A PLANE

NO WAITING
AROUND AT
THE AIRPORT

ZERO RISK OF
A PLANE CRASH

NO FULL-BODY
SEARCHES

NO NEED TO
FASTEN YOUR
SEATBELT

NO JET LAG

HIJACKING IMPOSSIBLE

SOME BOOKS ARE SUCH **PAGE-TURNERS** THAT YOU CAN'T PUT THEM DOWN UNTIL YOU'VE FINISHED! HERE'S THE **IDEAL EQUIPMENT** YOU NEED TO READ A NOVEL IN ONE SITTING

A DIAPER SO YOU DON'T HAVE TO STOP TO GO TO THE BATHROOM (NO MATTER HOW OLD YOU ARE)

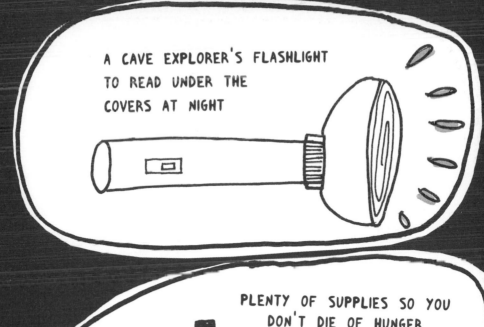

GREAT! NOW YOU CAN READ FOR **SEVERAL DAYS** WITHOUT STOPPING

A LITTLE SUGGESTION
TO AVOID BEING DISTURBED
BY STRANGERS WHEN YOU
WANT TO BE
COMPLETELY ALONE

CHOOSE YOUR BOOK TITLE WITH CARE!

METHOD TRIED AND TESTED
ON THE BEACH, BUS, AND TRAIN,
AND OUTSIDE CAFÉS

HOW TO
SCARE AWAY
PEOPLE WHO
COME
NEAR YOU

YOU DON'T EVEN HAVE TO READ...YOU CAN
JUST SNOOZE OR DAYDREAM BEHIND YOUR BOOK

WHICH OF THESE TWO PRESENTS WOULD YOU PREFER?

CHOOSE BETWEEN

(1)   (2)

 AN UNLIMITED SUPPLY OF STRAWBERRY GUMDROPS

 THE COMPLETE PHILOSOPHER'S DICTIONARY

 **+**

A DREAM VACATION ON A DESERT ISLAND

 +

A CONCERT TICKET TO SEE YOUR FAVORITE BAND

+

 THE GIRL OR BOY OF YOUR DREAMS

REMARK:

IF YOU CHOOSE PRESENT NUMBER ①,
NO MATTER HOW OLD YOU ARE,
YOU ARE DEFINITELY NOT NORMAL.
THERE'S MORE TO LIFE THAN READING!
MAKE AN APPOINTMENT TO SEE YOUR DOCTOR...

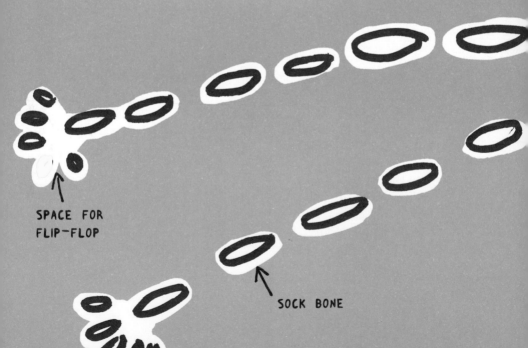

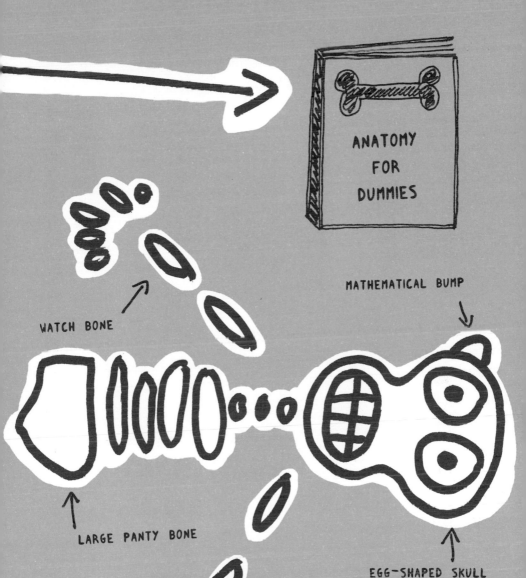

ANATOMY
FOR
DUMMIES

MATHEMATICAL BUMP

WATCH BONE

LARGE PANTY BONE

EGG-SHAPED SKULL

FINGERS FOR MAKING RUDE GESTURES

V.G.I.
(VERY GOOD IDEA)

IF YOU DON'T LIKE READING, **JUST** TAKE A BOOK TO BED WITH YOU: IT WILL GIVE OFF MAGIC VIBES ALL NIGHT

PROOF

ONE EVENING...

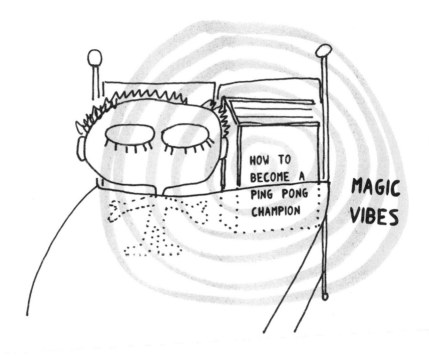

AND THE NEXT MORNING...

YEAH, RIGHT ⟶
(WINK, WINK)

LOTS OF READING:
1. IMPROVES YOUR CHANCES OF BECOMING RICH AND FAMOUS
2. WILL PUT YOU ON TV AND ON THE COVERS OF MAGAZINES
3. MEANS PEOPLE WILL ASK FOR YOUR AUTOGRAPH IN THE STREET

SHORT COMMERCIAL
BREAK

BUY SOME
MAGIC GLASSES

TO EASILY UNDERSTAND THE MOST
COMPLICATED BOOKS IN THE WORLD!

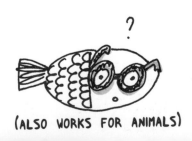

(ALSO WORKS FOR ANIMALS)

THE OLD,
CURIOUS
COD

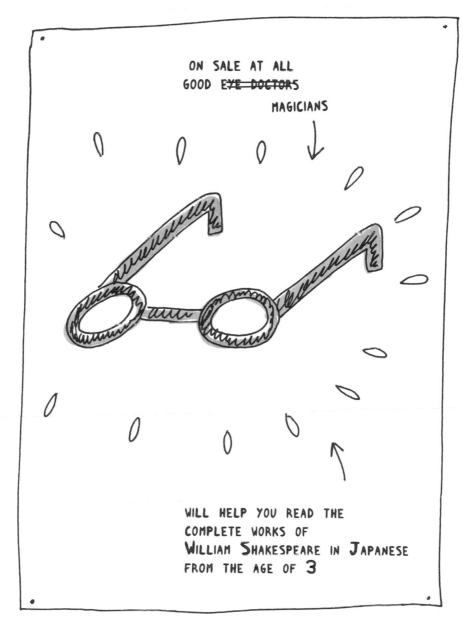

ON SALE AT ALL
GOOD ~~EYE DOCTORS~~
MAGICIANS ↓

WILL HELP YOU READ THE
COMPLETE WORKS OF
WILLIAM SHAKESPEARE IN JAPANESE
FROM THE AGE OF 3

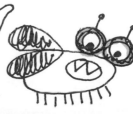

IF YOU OCCASIONALLY HAVE TROUBLE GETTING TO SLEEP, A **REALLY, REALLY BORING** BOOK WILL HELP YOU TO DOZE OFF

NO MORE
NASTY MEDICINE

NO MORE
SLEEPING PILLS

NO MORE
COUNTING SHEEP

HINT

HOW TO COPE WITH BOOKS

EVEN IF YOU DON'T LIKE READING

1. Choose a book
2. Close your eyes
3. Imagine that the book is a
YUMMY CHOCOLATE CAKE
with **YOUR FAVORITE TOPPING**
4. Pretend to nibble a little slice every day
5. When you've finished, choose
another book and imagine it's a
GIANT 12-CHEESE PIZZA

NOTE:

REMEMBER TO OPEN YOUR EYES BEFORE YOU
TAKE A BITE. OTHERWISE IT WON'T WORK

HAPPY READING!

YUM!

YUM!

1 SLICE = 1 CHAPTER

SO WHAT CAN YOU DO WITH A BIG PILE OF BOOKS IF YOU HATE READING?

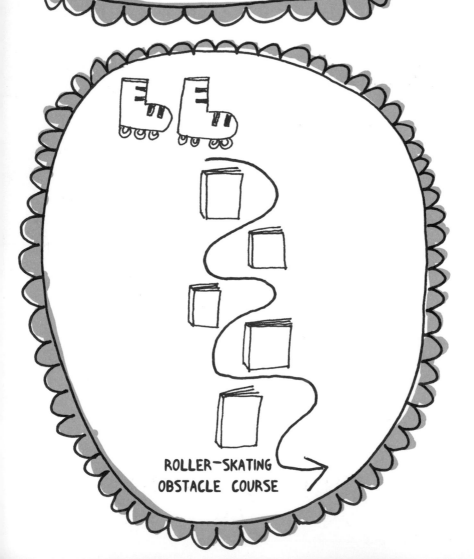

ROLLER-SKATING OBSTACLE COURSE

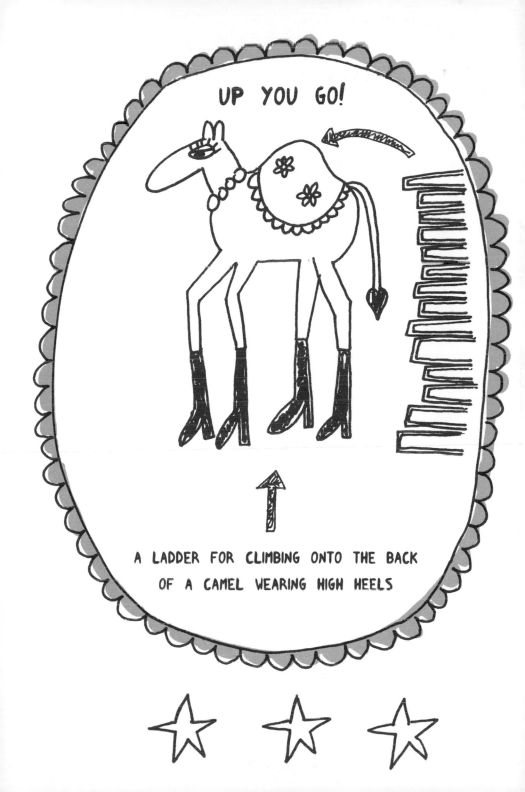

WHEN A BOOK IS **ABSOLUTE** AND **TOTAL TRASH** (AND ALL YOUR FRIENDS AGREE) YOU **CAN** DO THE FOLLOWING THINGS, WHICH ARE NORMALLY **FORBIDDEN**

MAKE CONFETTI

MAKE A BOAT TO PLAY WITH IN THE BATHTUB

USE AS TOILET PAPER

MAKE A SQUADRON OF PAPER
PLANES SO YOU CAN FLY
TO LONDON FOR FREE

WARNING NUMBER 2

HOWEVER, IF YOU TRY TO CUT UP **THIS** BOOK,
YOU'LL GET A MEGA ELECTRIC SHOCK, WHICH WILL
LEAVE YOU LOOKING LIKE A BURNED SAUSAGE

FINALLY, DO YOU KNOW WHAT THE **REALLY GREAT THING** ABOUT BOOKS IS?

1. WAIT FOR IT, IT'S AWESOME...

2. EVEN IF YOU NEVER OPEN THEM...

3. THEY'RE VERY USEFUL AT MAKING **YOU LOOK INTELLIGENT** (EVEN IF YOU'RE REALLY NOT!)

1 SO, LEAVE SUPER-COMPLICATED
BOOKS LYING AROUND THE HOUSE

2 AND KEEP ON WATCHING YOUR FAVORITE
MIND-NUMBING **TV** PROGRAMS!

LIFE'S GREAT, ISN'T IT?

SO THAT'S IT, FOLKS, YOU'VE REACHED
THE END

BUT DON'T BE SAD BECAUSE NOW YOU CAN
DO LOADS OF INTERESTING THINGS LIKE:

REALLY AMAZING IDEAS

↓

- READ THIS BOOK AGAIN

- BUY A COPY FOR ALL YOUR FRIENDS

- READ ANOTHER BOOK BY THIS AUTHOR

- READ EVERY BOOK BY THIS AUTHOR

LESS AMAZING IDEAS, BUT NOT ALTOGETHER WRONG

↓

- READ A BOOK BY ANOTHER AUTHOR

- HAVE A HOT BATH

- HAVE A DOUBLE CHOCOLATE-CHIP ICE CREAM

- MAKE A PRANK TELEPHONE CALL

- THROW A STINK BOMB

Copyright 2011 by Editions Nathan, Paris, France
Original edition: Le livre qui fait aimer les livres même à ceux qui n'aiment pas lire!
Published in the U.S.A. in March 2014 by Walker Books for Young Readers, an imprint of Bloomsbury Publishing, Inc.
www.bloomsbury.com

Bloomsbury books may be purchased for business or promotional use. For information on bulk purchases please
contact Macmillan Corporate and Premium Sales Department at specialmarkets@macmillan.com

Library of Congress Cataloging-in-Publication Data available upon request • ISBN 978-0-8027-3743-4

Publisher, Nathan: Jean-Christophe Fournier • Art Director: Lieve Louwagie • Design: Cécile Chaumet
Proofreader: Christiane Keukens-Poirier • Production: Lucile Davesnes-Germaine • Photogravure: Axiome

Printed in China by Toppan Excel, Guangshou City, Guangdong
1 3 5 7 9 10 8 6 4 2